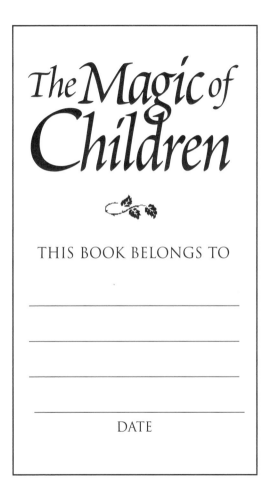

The Magic of Children

THIS BOOK BELONGS TO

_____

_____

_____

_____

DATE

The Magic of Children

A Celebration of Life, Love and Happiness

Dr. Mark Freed
Dr. Robert D. Safian
Photography by Kendra Dew

Physicians' Press

Text copyright © 1999 Mark Freed, MD
Photographs copyright © 1999 Kendra Dew
Cover and jacket design: Kathleen Brown
Production: The Lyle Group, Inc.

Library of Congress Catalog Number: 98-091745
ISBN: 1-890114-49-9
Printed in the United States of America
First Edition

Quotes and stories can be submitted
by mail, fax or e-mail. See page 139 for details.

This book may be ordered from the publisher by mail, fax, or e-mail,
but try your bookstore first! Please add $2.50 for shipping and handling.
Discount pricing is available for orders of 10 copies or more.

Physicians' Press
620 Cherry Street
Royal Oak, Michigan 48073
Fax: (248) 616-3003
www.magicofchildren.com

The Magic of Children Foundation

*W*hile *The Magic of Children* celebrates the irrepressible spirit of childhood, the authors' vision for the children of the world goes beyond celebrating and moves into action. To help young people with the many challenges that confront them, Dr. Mark Freed has established *The Magic of Children Foundation*, a non-profit organization dedicated to promoting the physical, social, and emotional health of children. In its initial program, *Adopt-a-doc*, doctors, nurses, and other health care professionals volunteer their time once a month to work with kindergartners through second-graders. Using the Foundation's curriculum, classroom materials, and student workbooks, *Adopt-a-doc* volunteers foster children's good health habits, personal safety, and self-respect. Dr. Freed expresses the Foundation's guiding principle when he says, "Love by itself is not enough—but the combination of love and *service* can change the world."

*I*f you would like to learn more about or become involved with *The Magic of Children Foundation*, you can either send us e-mail through our web site at **www.magicofchildren.org** or write to us at: *The Magic of Children Foundation*, 620 Cherry Street, Royal Oak, MI 48073

To our families with love, and
to our little friends with their big hearts,
for making every day feel warm and sunny.

And now, without further ado...

The Table of Contents

Our Staff

Henry
Age 4
*Vice-President
Strategic Planning*

Chrissy
Age 5
*Senior
Editor*

Jana
Age 1
*Customer
Service*

James
Age 5
*Ruler of the
Universe*

Introduction

*The best and most beautiful things in the world cannot be
seen or even touched. They must be felt with the heart.*

Helen Keller

Children move us in ways no one else can.
They make us laugh louder and cry harder
than any comedy writer or Hollywood tear-jerker.
They give us the strength to lift a car when their
safety is at stake. They remind us how to play
and how to forgive. They test our balance, our
endurance, and our tolerance. And as we clean up
their spills, straighten their bedrooms, and sit with
them under vaporizer tents, they teach us about
unconditional love.

The Magic of Children captures the essence of
children—their gentle innocence, eternal optimism,
and inimitable spontaneity and humor—and lets
you experience a rainbow of emotions. Feel the love

that flows from the award-winning photography of Kendra Dew as she captures the unbreakable bond between mother and child, and the delicate beauty of a little girl discovering her first sunflower. Revel in the laughter as you learn secrets about moms and dads, how long it takes to get to the moon, and what happens to you during sleep. And feel the joy and sorrow that only a child can inspire, as we share our own personal and professional experiences with you in the section titled "From the Heart."

The Magic of Children will stir up the inner child in you, reminding you of times when you spent hours looking for shapes in clouds and making angels in the snow, when your imagination turned a simple stick into a magic wand, and when messes and bumps and bruises meant you were having a good day.

We hope you enjoy this wonderful celebration of life, love and happiness, and that you share it with those you care about most. Your day will be brighter and your heart will feel lighter because of it.

Mark Freed
Robert Safian
Kendra Dew

Special Thanks

We would like to thank the many loving families who submitted their quotes and stories to us, and the many loving families who allowed us to reprint the photographs of their children in this book. You have given us all a very special gift.

We would also like to thank the following individuals for their important contributions: Norm Lyle, Tracey Daniels, Teresa Hartnett, Tina Johnson, Kathleen Brown, Brenda Anderson, Tom Borowiecki, Johanna Bierwirth, and the staffs at Quebecor Printing and National Book Network, especially Miriam Bass and Mark Cozy. You will always hold a special place in our hearts.

MOMMIES

Who ran to help me when I fell
And would some pretty story tell,
Or kiss the place to make it well.
My mother.

Anne Taylor

What's the difference between mommies and daddies?

"Mommies don't sit down when they eat dinner."

Jessica, age 4, one of five children under age 7.

"Mom, wouldn't it be great if the world was shaped like a heart? Then everyone would have to be *nice* to each other."

Randi, age 8, responding
to the violence on the
evening news.

What do mommies do?

"They care for you more than anyone else in the whole world."

James, age 4.

Tell me a secret about your mom.

"She sleeps with white paint on her face."

Rickie, age 6.

"Mommy, that lady needs to get some friends!"

Brianna, age 5, after listening to Celine Dion sing "All By Myself" on the car radio.

What makes you happy?

"When my mom comes home from work."

Jill, age 5.

A Moment to Remember

My husband and I were watching the end of a well-known Hollywood tear-jerker when my 18-month old son noticed I was crying.

After crawling into my lap and staring at me a few seconds, he gently touched his tiny finger to the tear on my cheek. Quickly grabbing a tissue from the end table, he gazed deeply into my watery eyes, and with a tender stroke of his sweet little hand, he softly wiped the tears from my cheek.

I held my son very, very tight as I cried all the harder.

What do you love most about your mom?

"The way she makes my toes tingle."

Ellis, age 3.

What can moms do that dads can't do?

"Say <u>No</u>!"

Gregory, age 3.

What does your mom do during the day?

"She complains."

Ben, age 3.

Gotcha!

I was in the kitchen preparing dinner when Brett, my 5-year-old, shrieked, "Mom, come quickly. I see a mouse!"

Before you could say, "Mom-to-the-rescue," I grabbed a broom, raced up two flights of stairs, and entered his bedroom.

"Where's the mouse?" I huffed, assuming a baseball batter's stance.

"Right there," chuckled my little imp, "attached to the computer!"

Food for Thought!

After returning home from a popular Middle Eastern restaurant, I had the following conversation with my son Brad, age 5:

"Sweetie, do you know what Mommie had to eat for dinner tonight?"

"What?"

"Baba Gannouge."

"Huh?" Silence and confusion.

"You know what else Mommie had?"

"What?"

"Falafel."

"Huh…?" More silence; more confusion.

"You know what else Mommie had?"

"What?"

"Hommus with Tahini."

"Huh…???" Total silence; total confusion.

"And do you know what else Mommie had?"

"Ummm…errr…uhhh…*diarrhea?*"

Hooray!

My daughter was 31/2 years old and extremely difficult to "potty train." Each time I would try to train her, I would give up, thinking she wasn't quite ready, and then try again in a month or two.

Somewhere between my fourth and fifth attempts, I took my diapered daughter to a very exclusive ceramic tile and bathroom shop.

As I was being consulted – and somewhat intimidated – by a sales associate with a heavy French accent, I heard a tinkling sound coming from behind me. I turned to find my little one, diaperless, next to a bathroom display, doing exactly what I had taught her, proudly clapping her hands together and singing "Hooray!"

The saleslady was less than amused, especially when *I* began clapping and singing as well.

My efforts to explain and offer to clean up the display were to no avail. I left without a purchase, but with a potty-trained daughter! *Hooray!!!*

DADDIES

He sings to me sweet lullabyes,
Protects me when I close my eyes,
And lifts me up so I can fly.
My dad.

Mark Freed

"Dad, do you always have this much trouble with *paralyzed* parking?"

Andrew, age 10, as his
dad held up traffic while
struggling to park the car.

What does the M.D. after your father's name stand for?

"My Dad."

Ryan, age 5.

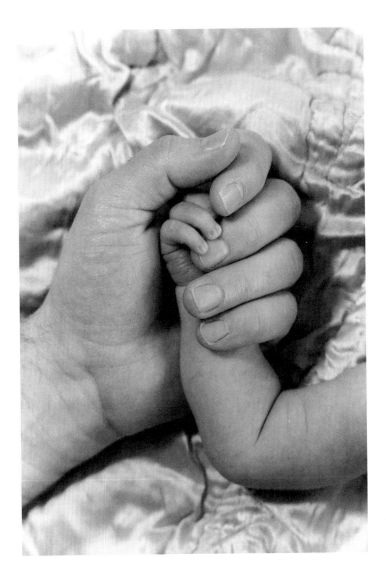

What does your daddy do during the day?

"He goes to work and plays with his big friends."

Jenny, age 4.

"My mom's is bigger
than the whole Earth and
my dad's is almost as big as
New Jersey."

*Luke, age 4, when
asked about the size
of the human brain.*

"Didn't you see one this morning while you were shaving?"

Brad, age 5, after his dad, a cardiologist, said he couldn't remember the last time he'd seen a doctor.

"Dad told Mom he's a *little horse!*"

Henry, age 5, about his
laryngitis-stricken dad.

GRANDPARENTS

There is only one perfect child —
And every grandparent has it.

"Why does Grandma always pinch my cheek?"

Bart, age 3.

Describe your grandma.

"Grandma looks just like me, except a little older.

Sarah, age 4.

What did you catch on your ice fishing trip with Grandpa?

"Pneumonia!"

Marv, age 5.

"Of course not, I'm going to leave it in the car!"

Ashlee, age 3, when asked if she was going to bring her blanket on her first date.

Tell me a secret about your grandfather.

"He can take his hair off his head and spin it on his finger."

Charlene, age 5.

"Don't worry Granny, I won't trade you in."

Johnny, age 4, after
Grandma spilled grape juice
on Mom's white carpet.

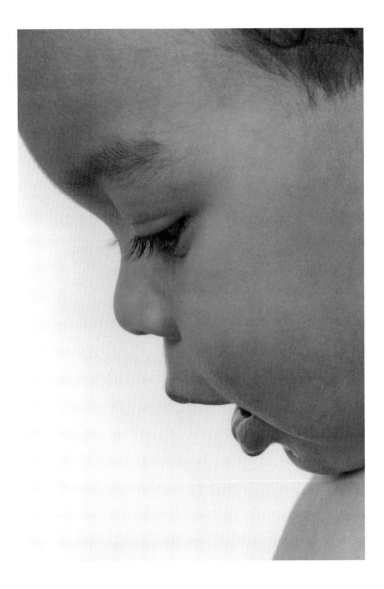

BROTHERS AND SISTERS

*The only time brother comes before sister
is in the dictionary.*

Susan Melnick

A Tale of Two Brothers

My daughter Suzanne was going out of town for the weekend, so she prepared gift bags filled with toys and snacks for her boys.

Johnnie, age 7, opened his bag first and found a ring. Little Mickey, the world's most competitive 3-year-old, quickly opened his bag and screamed, "You got a ring and I didn't!"

"But Mickey, you got a letter from Mom and I didn't," John said, trying to calm his little brother down. "Just think, you could keep the letter forever, you could frame it, you could..."

"But John," Mickey interrupted, "but John...but John..."

"But *what* Mickey?"

"But John," Mickey quipped, gazing dubiously at the letter, "I'm not even sure this is Mom's handwriting!"

Isn't that Pam's cracker you're eating?

"No, I already ate hers.
This one's mine!"

*Sarah, age 3, to her
Day Care teacher.*

A Conversation Between Sister and Brother...

"It is too."

"It is not."

"Is so."

"Is not."

"Uh-huh."

"Uh-uh!"

"Does so."

"Does not!!"

"Ya-uh."

"Nah-uh!!!"

*Nicole, age 4, and
Brian, age 5.*

HONESTY

Honesty is the best policy,
and children the best policyholders.

"Lady, you have a
gray hair in your nose."

Christine, age 5,
looking up at the
dental hygienist.

Would you like an ice cream sundae?

"No, I'd like it *today!*"

Megan, age 4,
to her waiter.

*How does a magician saw
a person in half?*

"Very carefully."

Norm, age 6.

LOVE AND MARRIAGE

*Love is a fruit in season at all times
and within reach of every hand*

Mother Teresa

How would you ask a girl to marry you?

"I am beautiful and you are beautiful so we should get married."

William, age 4.

Who would you like to marry?

"I don't know. I haven't met him yet."

Jackie, age 4.

How do you get a woman to notice you?

"Make 'Goo-Goo' eyes at her!"

Jay, age 5.

What is the secret to a happy marriage?

"Try to remember your wife's name."

Veronica, age 5.

TIME AND SPACE

*The only thing more vast than the universe is
a child's imagination.*

Robert Safian

*How long does it take to
get to the moon?*

"I think 1600 hours by
plane and 1700 hours by
helicopter."

Henry, age 5.

Where is heaven?

"North of Michigan."

Erin, age 4,
pointing south.

A CHILD'S VIEW
OF LIFE

The most beautiful view in the world —
life through the eyes of a child.

Kendra Dew

"It's sunny in my imagination, but it's cloudy for real."

Becky, age 4,
describing the weather.

What is your favorite nursery rhyme?

"Humpty Dumpty sat on a wall,
   Humpty Dumpty had a great fall,
   All the king's horses,
   And all the king's men,
   Ummm...*had scrambled eggs!*"

Christine, age 3.

What happens when you sleep?

"You close your eyes and spit comes out your mouth."

Sloane, age 7.

What do you want to be when you grow up?

"Captain of a big boat."

Jerry, age 4,
dreaming about life
on the high seas.

What is your favorite nursery rhyme?

"Row, row, row your boat,
Gently down the stream,
Merrily, merrily, merrily, merrily,
Life's about *ice cream!*"

Alexandria, age 5.

"By cutting corners!"

Mackenzie, age 4, on
how she saves money
using scissors and paper.

What is your religion?

"A boy."

Johnny, age 2.

"If at first you don't succeed, cry, cry again."

Joe, age 7, to his
younger brother, Andy,
on the secret to success.

If you could have one wish, what would it be?

"That I could have three more wishes."

Claire, age 4.

What do you want to be when you grow up?

"A kid."

Jodie, age 4.

FROM THE
HEART
(Stories from the Authors)

*Children refresh our spirit, make our
hearts smile, and give us the courage to
overcome overwhelming obstacles.
The following very personal stories capture
the joy and sorrow that only a child can inspire,
and remind us of what is really important
in life – health, happiness and love.*

Love's Resolve

I was the medical student on call the night a young family learned that Adam, their 7-year-old son, had muscular dystrophy.

It was 3:00 a.m. and I was making rounds before turning in. As I walked into Adam's room, I noticed his father, asleep in a chair, with a thousand-page textbook weighing heavily on his chest and a stack of medical journals at his feet. The man's lined face was ashen, his eyelids were swollen, and his reading glasses had slipped down his long, thin nose. The glow of the small lamp on the table beside him was the brightest light in the darkened room.

I put my hand on his shoulder and shook him lightly. "Hey, why don't you go home and get some rest?"

"No thanks," he murmured, as he sat up straighter in the chair. "I'll be fine right here." He picked up the heavy textbook, slid his glasses up to the bridge of his nose, and began making notes on the yellow, lined tablet in his lap.

"Are you a physician?" I asked, assuming by the textbook and journals that his answer would be yes.

"No," he replied. "I'm a construction worker."

Glancing up from his notes, he must have read the surprise in my face and the question in my furrowed brow. "Son," he sighed, "today I was told that my little boy has a crippling disease. That his arms, legs and spine will become progressively weak and deformed. That he'll be in a wheelchair by the time he's a teenager. That he'll probably die before he turns 20. And that there is no cure for his disease."

I learned in his next statement what real love is all about.

"You want to know why I'm reading these books?" he asked. "It's simple…" His voice faltered as his eyes welled with tears. "This is my *son*. My *boy*. My *life*. If the doctors can't find a cure, then *I will*."

A Child's Turn to Parent

I was 25 years old when my grandmother lost her vision to diabetes. Her husband and her sisters had passed away years before, and she was alone—except for my dad. Dad tried and tried to hire someone to stay with her, but eventually he had no choice but to move Grandma into a nursing home.

After 73 proud, independent years, she now faced a world of voices she did not know and beauty she could not see. It devastated her. When she started wearing her nightgown all day, I knew that her diabetes had robbed her of more than her sight—it had robbed her of her will to live.

My sister and I occasionally went with Dad to visit Grandma in the nursing home. We'd watch him feed her, and listen to her complain about the food and her stomach and her back and her teeth...and the strange voices in the night. Every thirty minutes or so, she'd ask if it was time for bed.

And each day, every day, after a long, grueling day of work, Dad sat by her side, feeding her dinner and false hopes that everything would be okay. Seven days a week, week after week, month after month, year after year.

He never talked about it. He was simply taking care of his mom, just as she had done for him when he was a child. But it was wearing him down. I saw it in the gray circles under his eyes and heard it in his weary voice. Yet, day after day, he went to the nursing home to care for his mom.

I remember the day—four years, three months, and thirteen days after she went blind—that she had her heart attack.

I met my father at the hospital. We sat by Grandma's side as she lay in a coma, listening to her labored breathing and watching the green lines on the monitor trace those interminable hours throughout the night. Her frail, delicate body fought to stay alive while at the same time it tried to let go. At 3:05 a.m., her heart stopped beating.

Dad and I hugged. Safe in our embrace, he wept. For the first time in my life, I watched my father cry. As painful as it had been for him to watch his mother suffer these past four years, he explained to me, it was nothing compared to the pain of losing her.

My dad has taught me so many things in life—how to read, how to throw a baseball, how to ride a bike. And yet, as much as I've learned *from* my dad, I cherish even more what I've learned *about* him.

The Littlest Santa

I t was Christmas Day in the Cardiac Intensive Care Unit—and it was busy.

The patients in Rooms 6 and 7 both had suffered massive heart attacks, and both needed heart transplants to survive. They were so weak and unstable that special equipment was needed to help their hearts circulate blood throughout their fragile bodies.

Ed Stanton was in Room 6. His robust frame and white hair reminded me of Santa Claus on this Christmas morning, but the 61-year-old man was really a janitor at a nursery school. I learned that he had been shoveling snow from his neighbor's driveway when his heart attack occurred—a typically selfless act, according to his children and grandchildren, who were spending Christmas morning with him. In the corner of his otherwise austere hospital room sat a small potted Christmas tree with brightly colored paper chains, strings of popcorn and cranberries, and white cutout snowflakes. The walls were decorated with dozens of Christmas and get-well cards, most of them done in finger-paints and crayons.

Richard Reynolds, the patient in Room 7, was a study in contrasts. He was 57 years old, a hard driving, highly successful executive who, in his words, "never really had time for family." The walls in his room were naked, his only company the intermittent swooshing sound of the medical equipment supporting his circulation.

As I started down the hall, I noticed Adeline, Ed's 5-year-old granddaughter, take a present from under the Christmas tree and walk into Mr. Reynolds' room, carefully sidestepping the wires and tubes and cords. "Merry Christmas," she said shyly, placing the brightly wrapped package on the edge of his bed.

Mr. Reynolds looked at her intently for a moment.

The swooshing noise of the machines seemed to grow louder. Adeline took a tentative step forward and pushed the gift a little closer to him. His tough exterior seemed to melt, and his face creased slowly into a smile. "Thank you, sweetheart," he whispered, reaching out with his well-manicured hand to gently touch her tiny fingers. "Thank you so much." I watched Adeline walk back into her grandfather's room, and then I glanced at Mr. Reynolds. He was pressing his forefingers to the corners of his eyes.

Mr. Reynolds died that night, despite the drugs and machines and my prayers. As his body was wheeled from the room, I noticed Adeline's gift, still in its original wrapping, with big blue teddy bears riding little green bicycles over pale yellow moons, all drawn and colored by hand.

Mr. Reynolds never opened his present, yet in my heart I knew it was the best Christmas gift he had ever received.

Hearts Touch

I was on my way home from the hospital after a long night on call. Lots of new patients. Lots of work. And, as usual, no sleep. I was weary to the bone and all I could think of was crawling into a warm bed.

It was snowing and bitterly cold that morning, but I was too tired to change out of my scrubs, so I threw on my winter coat over them. With my street clothes in one hand and briefcase in the other, I stepped onto the empty elevator.

On the way down, the elevator stopped on the obstetrics floor. A young mom entered with her newborn child cradled in her loving arms, followed by the proud new dad, who was juggling bouquets of flowers, handfuls of cards, and an "It's a Boy!" banner. They glanced at me to see if I noticed their baby, and then bent over the tiny bundle of love to coo, gurgle, and smile at him. I couldn't imagine two people being any happier.

The elevator then slowed to a stop in front of the Pediatric Intensive Care Unit. Another young couple stepped in, their arms around each other as they walked to the back of the elevator, turned, and stared at the floor. They were weeping.

The joyous couple looked at each other as the grieving couple moved behind them. Although the first couple couldn't stop staring in wonderment at their newborn, they fell silent. The other couple glanced furtively at the baby; the woman wiped her eyes and her husband swallowed hard as they tried to contain their despair.

The elevator bell rang as we reached the ground floor. The first mom shifted her baby to one arm, loosened a bouquet of roses from her husband's grasp, and handed it to the grief-stricken woman. Their eyes met briefly. Their hands touched slightly. The elevator doors opened and the two families went in opposite directions. No words were uttered. None were needed. The motherly love that both women shared created a lifetime of understanding.

The Five Most Beautiful Words

I was eight years old, a typical third-grader playing tag in the schoolyard during a typical lunchtime recess. Fifty yards beyond the schoolyard gate, several police cars with flashing red lights were gathered at the site of a car accident. A crowd of people surrounded the scene as one of the victims was carried on a stretcher and lifted into the ambulance. The teachers wouldn't let us poke our noses through the chain links of the gate, so I went back to playing tag, weaving and dodging so I wouldn't be tagged "it!"

The school bell rang, ending recess. I jiggled the handle of my locker to open it, grabbed my books, and sprinted to math class. There I spent the next forty minutes daydreaming about being a baseball player and an astronaut and a heart surgeon, all at the same time. A few hours later, on my way to history class, a friend stopped me in the hall and asked, "Hey Freed, how's your mom?"

"Huh?" I asked, confused.

"Your mom," he repeated. "The car accident…the stretcher…is she okay?"

"Oh my God!" I shouted, as I dropped my books, ran down the hall, crashed through the school doors, and bounded down two flights of stairs onto the sidewalk.

I rode the bus to school every day so I wasn't exactly sure how to get home. I just knew I had to. So I ran. As fast and as hard as I could. The houses, cars, and trees were a blur as I streaked past them, thinking only of my mom. *Up one street*—how she bundled me up in winter. *Down another*—how she bragged about me when she thought I wasn't listening. *Through an intersection*—the way she knew exactly how much peanut butter and jelly to put on my sandwiches. *Past a parking lot*—the loving way she looked at me when she thought I was asleep. *Across an alley*—the way she almost sang "Hi-i-i honey, how are you?" in her lilting voice when I'd come home from school.

As I hurdled a bush, I lost my balance and fell to the ground, badly scraping my knees and elbows. I knew I was bleeding, but I never stopped to look. I just kept on running as fast and as hard as I could, thinking about my mom all the way. *Down a side street*—the way she worried about me when I was five minutes late. *Across a lawn*—the way she laughed at my silly faces. *Around a garden*—how she knew I wanted help even when I was too stubborn to admit it.

My house came into sight. With tears streaming down my cheeks, I raced down the middle of the street, scared to death at what I might find. My heart was ready to explode.

Through the front door—did she know how much I needed her? *Up the stairs*—did she know how much I loved her? *Down the hall*—did she *know*?

I came to a halt at her bedroom door. Panting, I turned the handle slowly and opened the door a crack, just enough to poke my head in. She was lying in bed with her face badly bruised and bandages all over her arms. The room was full of family members and neighbors, yet she was the only one to hear me enter.

"Hi-i-i honey, how are you?" she called out, in loving concern.

Exhausted, I stumbled to her bed, hugged her gently, and whispered through my tears, "Just fine, Mom. Just fine."

I've been blessed with many wonderful friendships, many personal triumphs, and many professional accomplishments. But there has been no moment more special than when I entered my mom's bedroom thirty-two years ago and heard her say those five beautiful words, "Hi-i-i honey, how are you?"

And a Little Child Shall Save Them

It was a bright Sunday morning that reminded me of my childhood summers: the sound of birds singing, the caress of a soft breeze, the smell of freshly cut grass. While other people were packing picnic lunches, I was facing a busy day at the hospital—making rounds on twenty patients, dictating a dozen discharge summaries, and preparing six patients for surgery the next day.

I was perched on a stool at the nurse's station looking over patient charts when someone caught my eye. A little girl with fiery red curls and sky blue eyes, wearing a pink sundress with tiny red bows and pink and white sandals to match, was walking shyly toward me.

"Do you know where your mommy is?" I asked her. In response, she wrapped her tiny hand around two of my fingers and tugged me from my seat. I followed her down the hall, past the elevators, around a corner and down another long corridor, hoping she would lead me to her mother.

As we approached the Neonatal Intensive Care Unit, she came to a standstill and pointed to the big swinging doors. As I wondered what she wanted, she pulled a worn string of pink yarn from the pocket of her sundress and handed it to me. Then, in the sweetest, most tenderhearted voice I'd ever heard, she asked, "Can you help the sick babies?"

At that moment, a young woman came running toward us from down the hall. She heaved a loud sigh of relief as she reached us. "Emily, there you are, sweetheart. Mommy told you never to go anywhere without telling her first." In one loving motion—a move I could tell she had performed hundreds of times—she scooped up her daughter, kissed her cheek, and rested her comfortably on one hip.

"Thank you so much for finding Emily," her mother sighed, this time in appreciation.

After I explained that it was *Emily* who found *me*, I

told her about our journey through the hospital. She smiled knowingly at her daughter and clarified Emily's actions for me.

Emily's grandfather had been in the hospital all week with pneumonia. On their first visit, as they walked past the big doors of the Neonatal Intensive Care Unit, her mother explained to Emily that sick babies stayed in that room. On their twice-daily walk past the Unit, Emily would ask her mother to help the sick babies, and her mother would tell her that only doctors could do that. Today, Emily's grandfather was being discharged and her mother told her they wouldn't be coming back to the hospital.

"Sweetheart," said the mom, shifting her attention to her daughter, still on her hip, "did you go find the doctor so the babies would get better?"

Emily slowly nodded yes as she gazed deeply into her mother's face.

I blinked rapidly to clear my tears. Then I told Emily's mother how deeply I was touched by her daughter's humanity, and she smiled softly in acknowledgment. Her mood shifted to surprise as she noticed the piece of yarn in my hand. "Wow Doc, you should feel honored."

"Why is that?" I asked.

"Emily gave you her lucky pink yarn. She's never given that to anyone before."

I smiled warmly and said good-bye to Emily and her mom. As I walked back to the cardiology floor, I tied the small piece of yarn to my stethoscope, so that every time I examined a patient, I would remember little Emily and the beauty of compassion.

Love Everlasting

It was a slow night in the Emergency Room; the nurses were swapping recipes, the clerks were shuffling papers, and a few of my colleagues were arguing whether Michael Jordan was the greatest athlete of all time. I was just getting ready to take a catnap in one of the empty exam rooms, storing up on sleep in case things got busy, when suddenly they did.

"We have a 34-year-old woman in full cardiac arrest," shouted the chief paramedic, racing alongside the stretcher as a young woman was wheeled into the emergency room. "She lost her pulse and stopped breathing about five minutes ago."

Within seconds, the ER was in full motion. One nurse prepared the defibrillator, another quickly applied a blood pressure cuff, a third performed chest compressions. The woman's condition remained unchanged despite several rounds of drugs, electrical shocks, and a pacemaker.

"Call the surgeons. We have to open her chest," I barked, knowing it was her only chance for survival. Minutes later, I had the young woman's heart in my hand, squeezing and releasing, squeezing and releasing. All I could think of was that 34-year-old women are not supposed to die. I gritted my teeth. Squeeze and release. Still no change. Squeeze and release. Come on, *come on*. Squeeze and release. *Beat...pleeeease beat.* Squeeze and release. Squeeze and release... An hour later, we conceded defeat and stopped CPR.

Drained and disheartened, I accompanied the hospital pastor to the small conference room to talk to the family. I pushed the door open and was stunned to see only children in the room, six in all, ranging from preschool age to teenagers. I looked to the oldest girl, Anna, and asked her, "Where's your father?"

"He died in a car accident four years ago," she replied softly. "How's my mom?"

"Do you have a grandmother? An uncle? A babysitter?" I asked, grasping for names of adults who could help these children.

"No, it's just us. How's my mom?" she repeated anxiously. "Can we see her now?" followed one of the boys. "Does she have to stay in the hospital?" chimed the six-year-old.

I took a deep breath and gazed at the floor before telling the children I had some very bad news. Fumbling for words and trying not to stammer, I slowly and carefully explained how their mom's heart had stopped beating. I told them how hard we worked to save her life. And I told them that our efforts had failed.

The deafening silence gave way to a cacophony of sorrow. Two of the children fell to the floor kicking and screaming. Another ran wildly around the room, flailing his arms in excruciating pain. The others sobbed uncontrollably.

"No, no, it can't be true!" shrieked one of the boys, pulling on my labcoat and hitting me. "Mama! *Mama!*" screamed another child, over and over again. I stumbled from the room, my body numb, my heart broken.

Three days later, I sat quietly at the small funeral

trying to comprehend the children's immeasurable loss. My heart wept as Alexis, an eight-year-old girl with long brown hair and sad brown eyes, kissed her teddy bear and placed it tenderly next to her mother's grave.

After the service, I found my voice quivering as I told the children how deeply I grieved for them. Anna reached for my hand. "Thank you for trying to help our mom," she said softly, as a lump formed in my throat. "Mom may not be here to help us with our homework or make our lunch, but she'll be *here* forever" and pointed to her heart.

As I drove back to the hospital, my spirit felt refreshed by the young girl's inner strength, reminding me that love is everlasting.

Have A Story?

Hi friends! We hope you enjoyed reading *The Magic of Children* and shared it with a loved one. If you remember a funny, touching, or inspirational quote or story about a child or family, and you would like it to appear in our next edition, we would love to hear from you. Feel free to send us as many quotes or stories as you like. If you come across a wonderful quote or story in a magazine, newspaper, book, or newsletter, please send it to us as well. We will be sure both you and the author receive credit.

You can send your stories to us by mail, fax, or the internet:

By mail: Physicians' Press
　　　　　　Attn: The Magic of Children
　　　　　　620 Cherry Street
　　　　　　Royal Oak, Michigan 48073

By fax: (248) 616-3003

By internet: www.magicofchildren.com

The Magic of Children Website

Be sure to visit us on the internet at **www.magicofchildren.com,** where you can submit quotes and stories, learn about upcoming contests, and order this book.

Quotes & Photographs

Quotes & Photographs

Quotes & Photographs

Quotes & Photographs

Quotes & Photographs

Quotes & Photographs

Quotes & Photographs

Quotes & Photographs

Quotes & Photographs